FIELDS AND FENCING

by
Mary Gordon Watson

Illustrations by
Carole Vincer

THRESHOLD BOOKS

First published in Great Britain by
Threshold Books Ltd, 661 Fulham Road,
London SW6 5PZ

Reprinted 1990

© Threshold Books Ltd 1988

All rights reserved. No part of this publication
may be reproduced, stored in a retrieval system,
or transmitted, in any form or by any means,
electronic, mechanical, photocopying, recording
or otherwise, without the written permission of
the publisher.

Typeset by York House Typographic

Printed in England by Westway Offset

British Library Cataloguing in Publication Data
Gordon-Watson, Mary
  Fields and Fencing.
  1. Livestock: Horses. Grazing Management
  I. Title
636.1'084

ISBN 0-901366-66-8

CONTENTS

	4	Introduction
FIELDS AND FENCING	5	Fields – the four seasons
	6	A suitable field
	7	An unsuitable field
	8	Water and troughs
	10	Shelter
	11	Sheds
	12	Types of fencing
	14	Dangerous fencing
	15	Gates
	16	Field care
	17	Grassland
	18	Poisonous plants
	20	Health and condition
	22	The horse at grass in winter
	23	The New Zealand rug
	23	Catching a horse
	24	Check list

Introduction

It is more natural to keep a horse or pony in a field than to confine him in a stable, but not *every* horse will thrive living out at grass all the time, as conditions are seldom ideal and they are very different from his original habitat.

In the wild, he could wander freely to look for essential water and food, and to find shelter in very wet, cold and windy weather, or in strong sunshine. The natural grease in his ungroomed coat gave further protection against the elements, and also against flies. His travels kept his feet trimmed. A horse will seldom choose to be alone: he feels happier and more secure in a herd or paired with a companion.

However, without our help and regular attention, a horse or pony enclosed in a field would be deprived of many of these basic necessities.

In this book we show you how you can provide for your horse when he is turned out at 'at grass'. In particular, you will find that if you take good care of your field and the fences that surround it, you may avoid unnecessary accidents, disease, or other distress, and your horse is more likely to remain both happy and healthy.

Fields

A field, or paddock, or pasture, is an enclosed area of grassland where horses or ponies may spend up to 24 hours a day. It may be the only place available to them for food and exercise.

Many horses are limited to one small field which if grazed all of the time will soon become horse-sick and useless. It is much better to divide the area into three parts so that it can be grazed/treated/rested in rotation.

A minimum size of one acre per horse is a general rule, but this largely depends on the quality of the grazing and its management: weed and worm control, good drainage, applying fertilizer or other necessary treatment, periodic resting.

Field conditions vary greatly according to the weather and seasons.

IN WINTER, grass has no food value, and it may be frozen or under snow. Even the toughest ponies or horses, whether being worked or not, will need extra food to keep warm and healthy.

IN SPRING, the grass starts growing, and it is at its best from May to July. Horses must not eat too much too quickly.

SUMMER is a suitable time to rid a field of harmful or useless vegetation, to top or cut coarse, unwanted areas, and to harrow the land.

IN AUTUMN, the grass may grow a little, but if horses are standing about looking hungry they may need hay – and they will soon let you know how much to feed them.

A suitable field

The physical and mental well-being of any horse or pony depends very much on his surroundings. If he lives out in a field, his basic needs will be:

- A plentiful supply of fresh water.
- Nourishing grass, with extra food when necessary.
- Companionship – preferably with other horses.
- Shade and shelter.

A contented horse is unlikely to want to jump out of his field or chew the fences or trees or nibble at harmful vegetation because he is bored or hungry. He is also less likely to quarrel with his companions.

Most horses will benefit from a periodic change of field. New surroundings can prevent the formation of bad habits such as crib-biting, or walking up and down the fence.

Meanwhile, the 'used' field can be rested, treated if necessary, or grazed down by cattle.

Horses in a field should be looked over every day, and the fences should be checked. Any weak places, such as loose nails or wire, should be dealt with before they become a potential danger. Droppings should be removed regularly, and weeds pulled up and burned.

The quality of grassland can deteriorate rapidly, especially when over-grazed, and if it becomes horse-sick it will take months or even years of treatment and rest to restore its usefulness. Horses do not thrive on sour, foul-tasting pasture, or in muddy, bog-like conditions.

Good field management may take up more time and money but you will save on extra food, veterinary bills, and the effort it takes to get your horse fit.

An unsuitable field

A neglected horse in a neglected field is an ugly sight. It gives the horse owner a bad name – and he deserves it!

A captive horse is completely dependent on what he finds in his field. Water is vital to all his bodily functions. Dirty, contaminated water is not acceptable. It must be checked for dead insects, birds or other animals, leaves, or any unwanted matter. In very wet, cold weather, the horse needs shelter, and when it is very hot and the flies are troublesome he will need shade. A thick, bushy hedge is much better than an unsuitable shed.

A sick field will have bare, grazed patches and rough areas of inedible grass or weeds which horses will not touch. Harmful weeds and plants are a sure sign of bad management and unhealthy horses, and worm infestation from droppings is a severe problem.

Horses dislike being alone, but overstocking will soon ruin a field. Also, when they are hungry or bored they tend to fight.

If horses gallop about, for example when being chased by flies, or by each other, hazards to avoid include:

- Dangerous, weak, or inadequate fencing and gates.
- Any sharp objects that could injure a horse, such as nails, metal posts, barbed wire or wire ends, discarded machinery.
- Unprotected cables or pylons.
- Litter, such as bottles and cans thrown into the field.
- Rabbit holes, bogs, 'blind' ditches, or treacherous ground which may be too stony, slippery, or steep.

Water and troughs

Water is more essential to a horse than food. His body is 70 per cent water, and he needs between 5 to 15 gallons per day, according to the weather, his size and condition, and the moisture in the grass.

Water sources must be kept clean. Watch out for contamination from chemicals, insects, vermin, birds, algae, and leaves (never place a trough beneath deciduous trees).

Whatever trough or container is used, it must have safe, rounded edges and be strong enough to withstand hard kicks.

If a horse seems to prefer muddy, dirty water to fresh, he may lack minerals.

Ice in winter must be broken at least twice daily. Horses will not break it themselves.

A stream, with fresh, non-polluted running water, is ideal. It must have a firm, stony or gravel bottom, with easy access at all times of year, otherwise an alternative supply is essential.

A pond of stagnant (still) water should be fenced off. Such ponds are usually contaminated, boggy and dangerous. Only those which have a natural spring are suitable.

A badly positioned water trough, far too close to the gate, which is likely to become an extremely muddy area. Although it is useful to serve two fields at once, a projecting trough is potentially dangerous.

A water trough must have easy, safe access for horses, rounded edges, and no dangerous protrusions such as taps. It should be raised about 9 inches above the ground and fixed securely.

Automatic troughs are best, but make sure that horses cannot reach the ball-cock, and that the troughs do not become clogged with dirt, or flood. Pipes may freeze in winter unless lagged or buried deep in the ground.

An old sink, or similar container, is quite adequate provided the water is kept clean, fresh and in plentiful supply. Avoid using old baths, or anything sharp-edged, perishable, or unstable.

Portable water containers are useful for just one or two horses, but make sure that they cannot be pushed over. They are easy to clean and to move around when the ground becomes muddy, but they need constant re-filling.

Shelter

Horses need some form of shelter from wind, rain or sleet in winter, and from flies and sun in summer. This could be thick, high hedges or trees, walls, solid fencing, or a shed or building.

A hedge with overhanging shade is ideal protection against the elements, and horses often prefer this to a shed. Make sure, though, that it contains nothing poisonous. A belt or clump of evergreen shrubs or trees, such as holly bushes, also provides shelter and a good windbreak at all times of year.

If there is no shelter in your field, and if your horse is not a hardy type, you may have to bring him into a stable when the flies are troublesome, when it is very hot, or in extreme wintry conditions.

A high hedge is a good, natural windbreak which can also provide shelter and shade. Suitable varieties include blackthorn, hawthorn, beech, hazel and holly.

Trees can give useful shelter either in a fenceline or out in the field, whether it be one large single tree or a group or thicket. Low or dead branches should be removed for safety.

Solid fencing, banks and walls make an effective windbreak. If they are high enough on all sides, and well maintained, they give some protection from driving rain and sun.

10

Sheds

A field shelter which is strongly constructed to withstand all weathers and knocks will need minimum maintenance. It should be built on a dry, well-drained part of the field, with its rear wall against the prevailing winds. Its floor should be porous. (Deep litter bedding is suitable and it can be put down on to a natural earth base.) The doorway must be high and as wide as possible, to encourage horses to use the shed without fear of being trapped in a corner by another horse. The area around the entrance could be concreted if the ground tends to be very deep when wet.

A shed is useful, too, for feeding hay, out of the wind and rain, but most horses will only use it if it is light and spacious. A shed for two loose horses should measure at least 16 feet × 12 feet.

A shed, part-walled at the front against wind and rain. The wide doorway provides a safer escape route for a bullied or timid horse. It is bedded with straw which should be kept clean.

An open-fronted shed of simple and sturdy construction. Note how the roof slopes downwards to the back so that rain water is channelled away behind the shed.

Types of fencing

The fencing around a field or paddock must be safe, strong and high enough to contain horses. If it is lower than the height of a horse's back, he may be tempted to jump out, or he may lean on it with his chest which could weaken or break it. The gap between the lowest rail and the ground should not be more than 12 inches, so that a horse cannot roll underneath or become wedged. In spring and autumn, when their coats are changing, horses will rub hard against anything convenient such as posts or gates. Posts will last a long time only if they are of good-quality hardwood timber and sunk deep in the ground one-third of their total length. All rails should be attached to the *in*side of the posts, for greater strength and a smooth, safe fence-line without sharp angles or protrusions. Wooden fencing should be treated regularly with preservatives.

Posts and rails are long lasting if made of good quality wood and well maintained and preserved. Two strong rails are adequate, but three, as well as being higher, are better for enclosing small animals.

Plain wire with a top rail is a practical type of fencing and less expensive than an all-timber fence. The rail makes it easier to see, safer and more attractive. Strong posts are essential.

Plain wire is not ideal. It can cause cuts and injuries. Wire may stretch, so straining posts are needed to keep it tight and safe for horses. Wooden posts are preferable to unyielding metal or concrete.

A high, thick, **natural hedge** provides excellent fencing as well as shade and shelter. To be stockproof it should be at least 5 feet high, and 2 feet wide at its base.

Most hedges have weak places which livestock could push through. These need to be lined with a timber or wire fence. A hedge containing yew, privet, box, laurel or rhododendron *must be fenced off*.

A natural **bank and ditch** (*top*) may not keep horses in their field. A tight strand of wire secured to posts is a sensible precaution.
Dry stone walls (*bottom*) make excellent fencing if high enough and well maintained.

Plastic fencing (*top*) looks solid, is flexible yet strong, needs little or no maintenance and does not rot, rust, crack or peel.
Electric fencing (*bottom*) is useful for dividing a field.

Dangerous fencing

A horse owner is responsible for any damage that a horse does to himself or to others if he gets loose: so it is most important for animals to be safely contained in their field. Horses, especially young stock, are likely to collide with field boundaries when they are galloping about excitedly. Whether caused by boredom, stinging insects, or simply high spirits, accidents at grass – such as a broken leg, cuts, severe bruising, or loss of eyesight – are all too common. Leaving barbed wire fencing and strands of old, loose, loopy, coiled or tangled wire in a horse's field is obviously asking for trouble. A strand of wire fencing set so low that a horse could easily catch his foot in it is equally dangerous. Wire must be at least 18 inches (46 cm) above the ground. Other hazards include prominent nails, metal stakes and broken or weak timber.

If you cannot avoid using **barbed wire** fencing, at least make sure that it is tightly strained, with no loose, broken or very low strands. It is likely to cause jagged, often serious wounds.

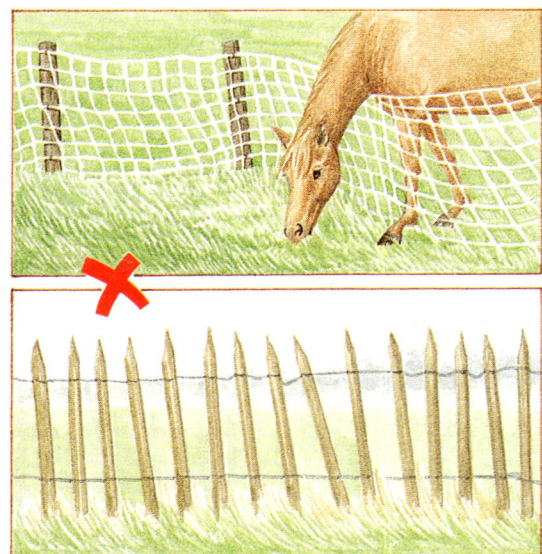

Pig/sheep netting (*top*) **chestnut paling** (*bottom*), or any other type of fencing which could trap a foot, leg, or even head, or might stake or otherwise injure a horse, is unsuitable and dangerous.

Weak fencing and dangerous gaps invite escape and disaster. It is preferable to use strong timber reinforcement – never barbed wire, metal objects, branches or rope which will be chewed.

Gates

A field gate must be sturdy, safe, and high enough to be horse-proof. It should be easy to open and close with one hand, and it must not swing. It is better for a gate to open *into* a field, to prevent horses or other live-stock bursting it open with their chests when you unfasten it.

As horses may often wait at the gate, pawing impatiently or perhaps biting and bullying one another, they could put a foot or leg between the bars. It is therefore essential to have a gate which is designed for horses, with no sharp angles which could form a trap, causing panic and injury.

A heavy wooden gate will sag unless it is expertly hung on very strong concrete-based gate posts. Tubular or galvanised metal gates are lighter and need less maintenance.

A wooden gate: strong, safe, well hung, and therefore easy to open and shut without dragging on the ground. All types of **catches** should be horse-proof, with rounded edges to minimise the risk of injury.

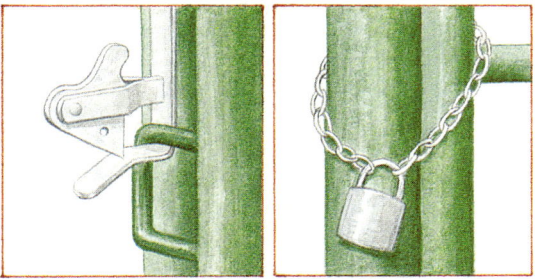

A suitable **galvanised iron gate**. In some areas it is a wise precaution to **chain** and **padlock** a gate – preferably at both ends so that it cannot be lifted off its hinges.

A bad gate: too narrow, not secure, with a sharp-edged gatepost and a prominent catch. If a horse bangs himself in a gateway he is likely to become gate-shy.

15

Field care

Fields which are over-grazed and neglected become 'horse-sick', with bare patches eaten down and areas of long but useless grass. When a horse eats the eggs of worms which live in droppings he becomes infested. If he lives in the same field continually it will ruin the pasture for future use. To make good use of limited grassland it is therefore necessary to rest, treat and fertilize it periodically. A field which becomes boggy needs artificial drainage.

Coarse, unwanted clumps of grass should be pulled up, cut down or, alternatively, grazed by cattle. Skill is needed to harrow, roll or spray a field. In bad cases ploughing and re-seeding may be the only way to make a field healthy again. By dividing it up and grazing it in rotation, problems can usually be avoided.

A harrow spreads fertilizer and breaks up droppings, killing off worms and parasites. Use it in dry weather. It also aerates the ground so that sun, air and rain can bring benefit to it, and fertilizer can be washed in.

A roller firms and strengthens pastureland and helps to level poached areas. It can be used about one week after harrowing – and always slowly, as it must not bruise the ground.

A cutter/bar mower/disc/rotary mower is used for 'topping' nettles, thistles, and coarse grasses which horses will not eat. Remember, *dead weeds are poisonous* and must be removed from the field.

Grassland

Horses will only eat the grasses that they like. They will starve rather than eat sour, rank grass.

Thick, lush, bright green grass may look healthy and appetising to us, but horses often prefer shorter, less inviting grass. There is little nutritious value in high, mature grass, so it should be cut, or eaten back by cattle.

Very rich pasture containing a lot of clover or alfalfa can be harmful to some horses, especially the small, hardy breeds which are better suited to sparse but clean, well-cared for grazing.

Ideal horse pasture is palatable, hardy in winter, digestible, resistant to hard grazing and cutting, and has varying peak flowering times. Herbage plants are most nutritious when young and tender.

Good grassland is rich in calcium and minerals.

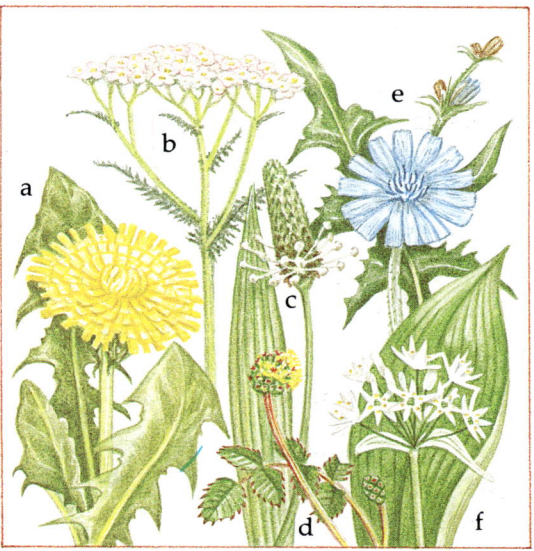

Palatable herbage: (a) Dandelion. (b) Yarrow. (c) Plantain. (d) Chicory. (e) Salad burnet. (f) Ramsons (wild garlic).

A good mixture of grasses: Rye grass. Cocksfoot. Timothy. Meadow fescue. Sheep's fescue. Bent grass. Purple moor. Yorkshire fog.

Poisonous plants

All fields should be kept free from harmful weeds and poisonous vegetation. Weeds such as nettles, docks and thistles rob the soil of its nutritional value and are signs of bad management. Although poisonous weeds such as chickweed, ragwort, or buttercups, do not taste good to horses they might eat them if they are very hungry, or eat the seeds mixed in with the grass. These weeds should therefore be pulled up by the roots and burned. In bad cases they should be killed with chemicals and the field vacated for at least a month. Above all, do not leave cuttings lying about: the wilting or dead plants become not only more palatable, but also much more poisonous.

Even the healthiest ground can become infected by neighbouring land, so check it as often as possible.

Common ragwort. Buttercup.

Hemlock. Woody, deadly and black nightshade. Thorn apple. Foxglove. Yellow star thistle. Bryony.

Shrubs: Oleander. Rhododendron. Castor oil plant. Laurel. Privet.

Trees: Yew. Laburnum. Acorn and oak leaves.

Horsetails. Bracken.

Health and condition

The behaviour and general condition of your horse must be checked daily. If you know how he is normally, you are more likely to spot an ailment soon enough to avoid serious results. If in any doubt, always call for veterinary advice: the horse may need treatment. Coughing, lameness, or a thin 'tucked up' appearance may be serious, while cuts and wounds need immediate dressing and could need stitching. Even horses out at grass without shoes need their feet trimmed every six weeks.

Not all horses or ponies are suited to being out at grass all the time, especially in extreme weather conditions or when flies are bad, but if they enjoy good grazing, a constant supply of fresh water and a safe, healthy field with shelter, they are less likely to be ill, lame, or injured. Prevention is better, easier and cheaper than cure!

To get the best out of your grazing, and to keep **worms** under control, pick up droppings as often as possible and worm all the horses in a field every six weeks.

Ringworm is highly contagious. As soon as you notice any small circular patches where the hair comes away, isolate the horse and handle him as little as possible.

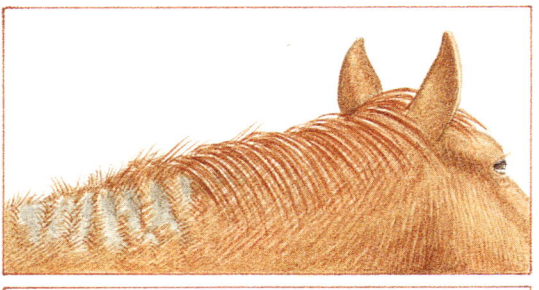

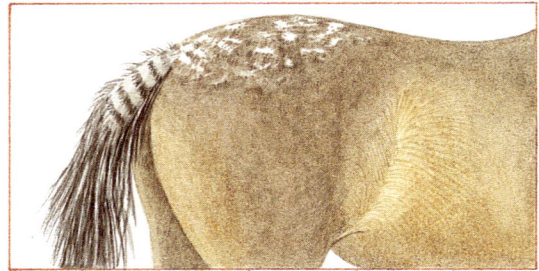

Mange (*top*) is an infectious skin condition caused by mites burrowing into the skin. **Sweet itch** (*bottom*) is an ugly, sore skin allergy, worst around the mane and tail, and probably caused by midge bites.

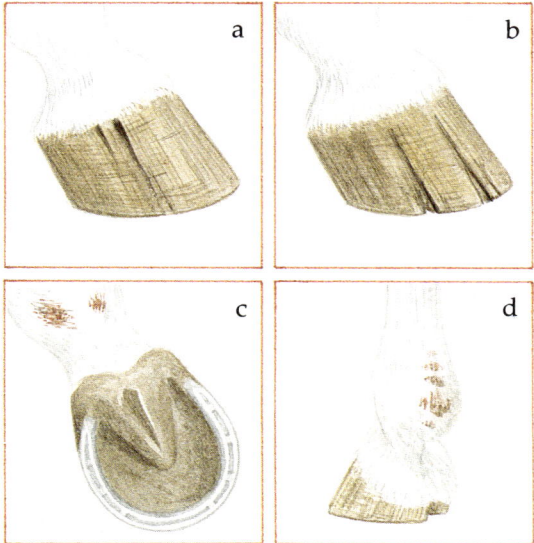

(a) **Sand crack**, (b) **grass crack**, (c) **cracked heel**, (d) **mud fever**. Neglected feet may lead to prolonged lameness. If mud fever or a cracked heel become infected treatment in a stable will be necessary.

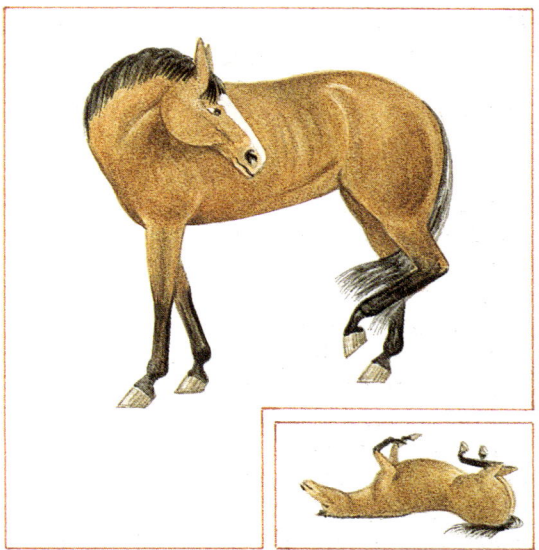

Colic, a stomach ache, has many forms and various causes, most of them avoidable. It often becomes serious, and the vet should be called immediately to diagnose the type of colic, and to treat it.

Laminitis (founder) is a painful fever in the feet which mostly affects small, fat ponies who have eaten too much lush grass. They will stand on their heels and be reluctant to move.

Crib-biting and wind-sucking are vices which often develop in a stable. They are caused by boredom, mental stress, or frustration at being over-confined, and may lead to digestive disorders.

21

The horse at grass in winter

Most horses adapt well to cold weather, provided they have enough bulk feed, water, and protection against driving rain or sleet.

From October to April, when the goodness has gone from the grass, they will need hay and a regular extra feed to keep them warm and in good condition. Feed them away from the gate, or fenceline, to avoid poaching the ground. Haynets or feeds should be spaced well apart so that shy horses are not intimidated by greedy companions.

If their water freezes, it must be broken at least twice a day, and the pieces of ice removed.

When grazing is not possible because the ground is too frozen or muddy, extra hay should be fed.

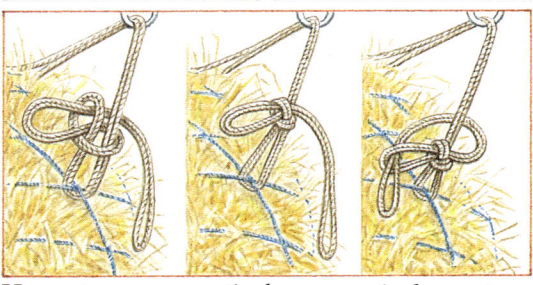

Haynets are a practical, economical way to feed hay. Secure them as above, high enough so that when they are empty a horse cannot trap his foot. Provide one net per horse, not close together.

Hay fed loose on the ground (*top*) is practical for large numbers, but it may be trampled into the mud, or blown away. A good **hayrack** (*bottom*) which can be moved if the ground becomes very poached.

Feed bowls and troughs should be strong. Do not use wooden boxes which may splinter, nor buckets which can tip over or split. Keep them clean and far enough apart to discourage quarrelling.

New Zealand rug

If your horse or pony is clipped, or feels the cold, or if you want to conserve his condition and energy, he will need a waterproof New Zealand rug – or preferably two, so that when one is wet through it can be replaced with a dry one and then be dried itself. A warm, dry horse will require less feeding.

Remember that any horse whose stomach has been clipped will not be protected by the rug on his underside, and he should have somewhere dry to lie down such as a stable or shed.

A well designed rug will fit the shape of a horse's back and is unlikely to slip round. It should be roomy at the shoulders to allow easy movement and grazing without chafing.

Catching a horse

Horses are sensitive to sudden noises and movements, and even to strange smells or clothes, so never shout or be aggressive if you want them to trust you and let you handle them.

To catch a horse, take a headcollar and rope, and a titbit (carrot, sugar lumps, nuts, apple) to the field, remembering to close the gate behind you. If he lives alone, try calling him, but if he is among others, approach him from the front and side, and speak to him. Offer the titbit with your left hand, and slip the rope around his neck with the other hand. While he is eating, put on the headcollar, and reward him again.

To catch a nervous, headshy, or workshy horse will need patience and tact, or he may follow his companions to the gate. If being caught is a pleasant experience, you should have no trouble.

Check List

REMEMBER . . .

Some horses do not thrive when living out, exposed to extremes of temperature, rain, mud, insect bites, bullying. Others become bored or lonely after a few hours. Sometimes it may be necessary to combine field and stable life to keep them happy.

If your horse or pony does best out in a field, or if there is no choice, you can at least make his life as pleasant as possible.

A happy horse is easier to look after, and a pleasure to own, whereas a discontented, unhealthy horse is not!

FIELD CHECK

- Constant supply of fresh, clean water.
- Healthy grass – plenty to eat.
- Eliminate weeds, worms, poisonous plants.
- Adequate shelter and shade.
- Safety – no holes, litter, sharp objects, loose wires.

FENCING CHECK

- Safe, secure gates. Padlock (where necessary).
- No weak spots.
- No protrusions or hazards: nails, broken wire/rails.

VISIT YOUR HORSE EVERY DAY